Table of Contents:

Foreword

This is the strange and yet factual story of an American soldier's voluntary involvement in a mission to provide training to Montagnard Tribesmen in their villages somewhere in the mountainous terrain of Vietnam near the Laotian border. It has been more than fifty years since the mission took place, and with the secrecy recently lifted on the story it can now be told by one of the few persons involved. The paragraphs below chronicles a virtually unknown part of the intrigue and courage associated with a Central Intelligence Agency (CIA) operation that simply did not or could not function as it was intended to do.

Later research indicates that the operation probably involved persons by the hundreds, mostly young soldiers, and by early 1961 the death rate was approaching the point of raising suspicions by distraught mothers and the American press. It was then that the CIA decided to send Japanese War Criminals, labeled as advisors, to perform this risky undertaking. Unfortunately those efforts failed miserably, with the Japanese Advisors simply disappearing from the face of the Earth and in a similar manner to the American soldiers. Not even one of these so-called Advisors is documented to have ever been seen or heard from again.

The very legitimacy of his having waited eight years after obtaining a copyright to finally release this account, exposes the fact that he still retains inner concerns. For this reason he has insisted that his name be changed to identify him as Arie Stone and not to reveal his given name.

Due to modern forensic techniques involving iris and facial recognition, the accompanying photos have been altered to make the task of identification more difficult although not impossible.

Chapter One: Looking for answers

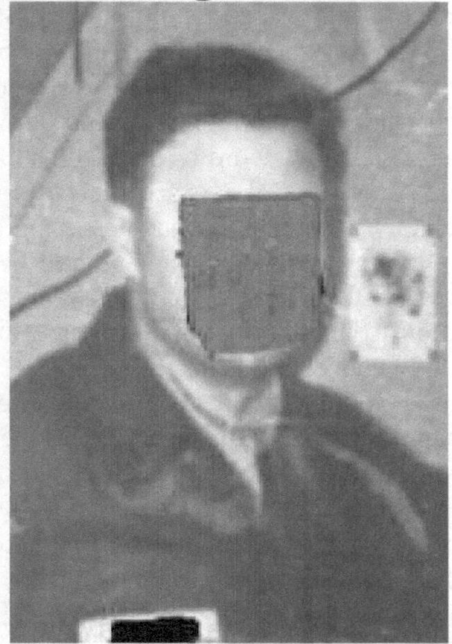

A short time after Arie began his research, some evidence was released showing the US involvement in Laos and Viet Nam began during the Eisenhower Administration and as early as 1954. During this time, multiple US efforts were imposed upon Southeast Asia and with little or no fanfare by the major news agencies of the day. Although the efforts were covert, those efforts could have quickly been identified and the information easily recovered. The US originally intended to provide aid to the French Military in their fight against the Vietnamese resistance, however the US continued the encounter long after the French had left the field of battle and in fact had returned home. Few persons cared about the activities in this part of the world and most Americans would not become familiar with the names of Vietnam and Laos until the 1964 Presidential election or later.

At any rate, reports released fifty years later indicate that the use of the American troops did not work out as planned by the CIA. How many years and how many deaths are attributed to this ungodly operation, no one is accurately presumed to know.

One of the Japanese Advisors was a Colonel named Masanobu Tsuji. He was a fanatical Japanese militarist that was hunted after World War II for complicity in the Bataan Death March among other dastardly actions. For a reason unknown to this day, around 1958 the CIA and US Army files indicate that he began working for US Intelligence. A few years later in 1961, he mysteriously vanished while in Southeast Asia and he was never to be seen again. His family waited years for word of his whereabouts, but it was all in vain. Unlike the brave American Soldiers sacrificed on previous missions of this type, he most probably suffered a just and deserving fate.

The soldier in this story knew back then that if he was ever to publish this story that he has worked on for nearly fifteen years, it could certainly be an unpleasant revelation to his children and siblings, so that is why he has chosen to remain in the shadows to this date.

This self-assured soldier, and possibly some other persons, believe it can be rightfully assumed that all the American Troopers vanished or were killed shortly after being dropped off at their assigned destinations. Perhaps they were led into the woods and their lives traded to the Viet Cong for rice and weapons. Regardless of the circumstances for their demise, it appears quite obvious that all the soldiers were eliminated within a few hours or days of arrival at their mission objective. In any event, it is quite apparent that these daring American soldiers were mere pawns of the CIA, and that multiple groups of these unsupported Military Trainers were solitarily and repeatedly thrown at the Montagnard problem in hope that something might work.

After a long series of plying failure upon failure, and always with disastrous replication, the CIA finally realized in late 1961 that the single-soldier cornerstone for such training was not an answer to helping the Montagnards improve the overall Vietnam situation. It was at this time that President Kennedy announced the creation and use of Special Forces within the Montagnard compounds. What was not revealed was that these superb and well-trained troopers, known as Green Berets, would be sent in as twelve-soldier squads rather than the solitary trainer. Whether this was done due to the situation having escalated, or because a single soldier could not possibly accomplish the task, is unclear and not well documented. It is believed to have been due in part to the US Army, with its large resources, taking over all command of the Vietnam situation from the thinly staffed CIA personnel. However it is well substantiated and fully known that in 1964, one Montagnard village rebelled prior to killing 80 South Vietnamese soldiers and taking 20 Green Berets hostage. Thankfully those hostages were later released unharmed. Nonetheless it is apparent from the reports that at the time of this atrocity there were a hundred Military Advisors stationed in that single out-of-the-way village and this appears to be confirmation that the solitary soldier concept had long since faded from the realm of possibilities, if it was ever considered viable at all.

For the many years following this *CIA Mission to an Internal Hell,* this loyal American was taken down self-destructive paths on numerous occasions that could have easily resulted in his death, imprisonment or being institutionalized. Time and again he would go off alone in the dark, to remain in hiding from his family. There he would sit quietly with his eyes misty and the great weight of what he believed was his tarnished image coming down around him, for he believed he should feel ashamed of his survival. All the while this trepidation continued to become an ever-larger part of his life that no one in his family ever knew about even to this very day.

Chapter Two: Wanting to be Involved

Here is the shocking beginning of something that only God knows how it will end. It was shortly after his nineteenth birthday that this all started, and Arie was in excellent mental and physical health. While he is not the equivalent of rocket scientist material, the Army did measure his IQ at 137, which placed him far above the average soldier. Since then, he has worked his way through three colleges while was working full time to support his family. It was during this period that he attained three degrees including one in law from a prestigious university in California, with the latter being obtained in only two years rather than the usual three years. He says this not to brag, but to explain that he does have acceptable powers of reason on most subjects, except for the shadowy bits and pieces incurred during this single incident—an incident of multiple blurs that are trapped deep within his own mind. Further, he does not believe that it is because his memory has fogged too much with time, although of course it is a possibility.

Now before he gets too deeply into the account, you are assured that he is not and has never been in a mental institution, except while studying patients during his pursuit of a psychology degree at a renowned State University in the Southwest. Further he is proud to say that he quit smoking in March 1961, and he quit drinking in August 1985. In addition there is no time within his life when he took drugs of any sort, except a few prescriptions for short periods. All in all he believes he could be described as a health nut by some persons!

During the time he achieved his law degree, he dedicated a large sum of time to the checking of all available sources within the US Army via the Freedom of Information Act (FOI) and found very little supportive documentation of his actions as identified in this narrative. Further, there is no written verification of this particular mission available to him or to the public in general that he has been able to locate.

Arie soon realized that his military records are merely a simple and rather mute testimony to an average soldier doing an average tour of duty in the relative calm of the Far East. Those same records do not reflect any of his Army Reserve time or any of what he is saying in this explanation, except for one new revelation. After 30 years of FOI requests, a new document has recently surfaced and it shows an undated entry for his *Counter Insurgency* training while with the Military in Korea. This is strange entry since the term counter insurgency was not a part of the standard military jargon at the time of his service. While there are frequent references to his Counter Infiltration training, most of the soldiers stationed with him would have had no idea what was meant by the word *Insurgency*. To his best recollection, he had never received any training of any type that was identified at the time as Counter Insurgency.

FOI request forms that were sent to the CIA came back with an emphatic *no record*. This is not surprising, due to their refusal even to admit *their* own existence. However it did bother him emotionally, for he knew there was something concrete that was being concealed. He has always prided himself on remembering places and dates. To this day his older siblings often call him to clarify an occurrence or a date, and some of their requests go back before his fifth birthday.

You may be wondering why, as an attorney, he has not sued them and the answer is very simple indeed. This is the *only* incident in his entire life that he cannot state to any degree of certainty truly happened to him. The snippets that he does remember have left a good portion of the happenings cloudy as to belie their possible authenticity. Yet the outer fringes of the episode remain with him and in such minute clarity as to dismiss any idea of misperceptions. This entire incident has left him with few answers and a vast amount of questions, including the biggest one of all: did it really happen? Yes, he truly believes it did take place and that is the reason behind his willingness to come forward with his story.

Further Arie believes his mind is quite acute and he would be much more knowledgeable of the facts except for the CIA's use of a new drug that would later be known as LSD. Still from the very day this episode transpired until this point in time, he can remember the facts as merely a bunch of components with key and vacant gaps in between them. However, the many details of his life before this incident, and in the fifty years following, are perfectly clear with no gaps or voids in his recollections. In fact he even remembers the vivid minutiae of encounters that were on occasions scurrilous in nature, including a few he would certainly be fond of forgetting. Still in this telling of the account he will only reveal the pieces of the details that he remembers, and he will permit the reader to fill in the other parts with their own logic and analogy. He simply asks that you assess all the statements as provided in this explanation, and at that time make your own conclusions as to what occurred during the excursion into what he has come to label—*CIA Mission to an Internal Hell.*

Chapter Three: Arriving at Base Camp

It was shortly after daybreak on the morning of his nineteenth birthday that he waded ashore at Inchon, Korea. The year was 1960, and the weather was quite warm and humid. Tromping through the knee-deep mud to reach the shoreline, he was repeatedly muttering a well-known refrain. *"Happy birthday Arie! Happy, happy birthday!"* It was a balmy day and it was his first contact with the stench of Korea, but it would certainly not be his last.

In a short time, Arie was accepted by all the "old timers" that shared a Quonset hut, known warmly as a hutch. There were approximately thirty men to each hutch and within a few days, Arie was using the extremely dull hours to entertain and amuse the men.

Quickly snapping open his locker with such force that the door emits a bang that can be heard across the quadrangle below, he exposes the magazine fold out of a lovely young woman. “I know some of you have been away from the US for a long time, so I am taking this time to clarify a few things. Regardless of what you have been told, you are not fighting for God, Country or apple pie. This is why you are fighting! Now some of you may be asking *what the hell is that beautiful thing?* It is a woman! This person—or one very similar to her—is waiting for you back home. So chin up! There is light—and lovely young women—at the end of the tunnel!”

Immediately the troops began to laugh and talk, as the mood shifts from despair to a feeling of good times are just around the corner. While most newly assigned soldiers were depressed and depressing by their being in such an isolated part of the world, Arie was not the type. He believed in enjoying life as it is presented, and he was just what the group needed to lift their spirits.

In the months that followed, Arie was constantly making them laugh, even when bad situations were expected and rumored to become worse. He organized groups to go to the ECO club for drinks. He rounded up a few persons to accompany him to the nearby orphanage, when the boxes of candy were greatly appreciated. He wrapped Christmas presents for those solders that were all thumbs, and he volunteered for guard duty on Christmas Eve in order to allow a Jewish soldier to have a break. Although he was slightly younger than the rest, he was a highly-respected member of the group, even if he was one of the few without a college degree.

Chapter Four: On the DMZ

For an entire thirteen-month tour of duty, he was to be stationed along the Demilitarized Zone (DMZ) that divides South Korea from North Korea. Soon a wide variety of other tasks was assigned to him, with his most important and time-consuming obligation being to walk guard duty along the DMZ. For a while everything went fairly normal for him, although at times he was quite uneasy and almost fearful as he spent 24 hours out of every 72 hours walking alone through the brushy area of the border with North Korea. Rain, shine, blizzard or squall, he was required to be a solitary sentry all night and day in a very lonely space quite out of earshot of the other sentries. All the while he was feeling extremely vulnerable to any sniper-shot or would be assassin from the north side of the fence. During his many hours alone, the Sergeant-of-the-Guard only checked on him twice during his yearlong tour, and one of those times occurred just prior to nightfall at around 6 PM. It appeared to him that all those in charge were fearful of being along the DMZ after dark. Yet and despite everything, his youthful exuberance would not often allow him to be overly frightened for his life.

Isolated and feeling abandoned while on guard duty, he remembers that in the middle of a blizzard he once tried but could not see his own hand in front of his eyes. Then something grabbed him from behind and covered his face. His training instinctively took over and he dropped to his knees in an attempt to throw the person or thing over his shoulder! It was then that he realized it was only a newspaper. Nevertheless, he was quite shaken because he knew it could have just as easily been an enemy soldier.

Another time at around 3 AM, he was standing on a hill looking down into the foggy bottom land toward North Korea, when he noticed a soldier about 100 yards away and coming toward him. The person was utilizing the standard zigzag pattern of running a few yards, dropping down for a minute, and then getting up and running toward him again. Arie stood his ground and waited as he debated calling for the Sergeant-of-the-Guard or not. Deciding to remain quiet so as not to give away his location, he loaded a round into the chamber of his weapon, while holding the unlit flashlight in his left hand, then Arie put the flashlight on him and ordered him to halt. It turned out to be a drunken GI that had gotten lost while returning from one of the village hot spots. That GI sobered up quickly after Arie threatened to shoot him! In any event, after checking him for weapons, Arie sent him off toward the Guard Shack. It was then that his knees weakened to the point that he could not stand. Had it been an enemy soldier, his issue of only five rounds of ammo may not have been sufficient to save his life, given his poor marksmanship with the short-range carbine.

Nevertheless, the primary and biggest shock he received in Korea was the early arrival of winter. Winter in Korea begins much earlier than in the Midwestern United States and it began the first week of October with an overnight freeze that covered every exposed object with a coating of ice, including the leaves on the trees. This shook him, because he did not expect winter's arrival for at least another month, and his mind raced with the frightening possibility that if the days of early October were this bad, then the dreaded month of February would surely be unbearable. Arie had always hated February in the Midwest with its oppressive dampness and unrelenting cold. Suddenly, the quarter mile walk from the shower facility back to his hut had changed from merely a nuisance to become overtly dangerous, as the temperature seemed to hover around a minus 24 degrees for weeks on end. The definite idea the terrible cold instilled in him was to make him anxious to pursue all honorable options to leave Korea for a warmer assignment. This was especially true in light of the fact that his job was the only one that he knew to be deemed *indispensable*, and as such he was forbidden to receive the required allotment of a ten-day rest-and-relaxation (R & R). Although everyone above and below his rank took their R & R time, he was specifically prohibited from even applying for any R & R. He mentions this not to deride the other soldiers, but to help explain why he would later jump at the chance to leave his present assignment. It also raises the question of how anyone, while holding a classification of truly indispensable, could quickly be approved for immediate transfer.

That January was every bit as cold as he had feared it would be, and the anticipation of a much colder February was becoming even more disturbing to him. In spite of everything, there appeared to be no way of escaping the freezing onslaught, so he steeled himself to bear the unbearable.

Then in late January 1961, as though from an answered prayer, he was ordered to the headquarters of the Commanding Officer (CO). Waiting for him there was an unfamiliar officer holding the rank of Major. The Major did not issue an order, but rather asked him to take a seat so that they could chat. After the initial salutations, nothing more was said, until the Major was sure that the CO had left the room and that they were alone. In a low voice, the Major approached him about volunteering for an assignment. The mere word, *VOLUNTEER*, made him want to leap up and run from the room! It brought back memories of the first time the Army had asked him to volunteer. During basic training he had been asked to volunteer for the bacteriological prevention studies at Fort Meade, with his pay and his life insurance automatically doubled! He refused then and he had no doubt that he would refuse again, whatever this new assignment.

While watching every physical movement of Arie, the Major explained the mission as a super secret one. This matched the secret clearance of Arie and his past skills as a hand-to-hand combat trainer for the six months he spent as a temporary Sergeant in a basic training outfit. All that seemed like a long time ago, with basic training being considered a happy time compared to his situation today. The Major continued to explain that the mission was to train the backward Montagnard tribesmen in the mountains of Vietnam on the basic tactics of defense. Further he explained it was anticipated by Washington that such training would allow the Montagnards to protect their homes and crops from the many marauding Vietnam army deserters and turncoats. No mention was made of North Vietnam Regulars or of their Russian and Chinese counterparts. Neither he nor the Major had any doubt about his ability to do the job, and the only question was did he want to do so? He listened to the sales pitch, without knowingly showing any interest or even a lack of interest, but deep inside he was merely waiting for the appropriate time to say a firm, “Hell no."

The one thing that he did not ask the Major was about the duration of the mission, since he had only six months left on his military obligation and naturally presumed that the Major had thoroughly reviewed his records and knew this to be a fact also. Bored and yawning, he tried to appear interested as he asked the Major if it was warm there.

The officer excitedly replied, "Warm? Why there are palm trees everywhere! When you're not on training duty, you can sunbath or just relax in the shade, because the average temperature year-round is a balmy 80 plus degrees!"

Arie now knows that his eyes must have lit up similar to the neon lights of New York City, because he sat up straight in the chair and said without thinking, "You can sign me up!"

He was quickly informed that there was nothing to sign, as no document would be necessary to get him into his special group, and that he was to inform the other members of his current outfit that he was simply being transferred. The Major informed him that in three days an Army Staff car would pick him up at the main gate and take him to Seoul, where he would receive additional instructions concerning this new assignment.

He was amazed by the statement of the Major, since he was presently classified as indispensable and strictly forbidden to go on any R & R leave! Yet, the Major was implying that he could be replaced in a mere three days for this new assignment! Although eager to leave, inwardly he began to wonder if his CO would really consent to let him go that expeditiously.

The days that followed made it quite clear that there was to be no problem with his leaving, since his immediate boss, an affable First Sergeant from World War II, announced that he would gladly handle such tasks in addition to his own. This First Sergeant, with his full head of gray hair, his gray mustache and his false teeth, he looked and acted like everyone's grandfather, even though he was only 42 years of age.

Not unlike himself, this sergeant had entered the Army with every intention of putting in a couple of years and then returning home to settle down. A few times, he had told the story of the Battle of Corregidor and that it had happened while he was stationed there. By the time he was released by the Japanese at the end of the war, he had accumulated seven years of service, so he decided he might as well stay another 13 years or so and get his pension.

Being the senior man in the hutch that the Army called a barracks had allowed Arie to build himself a semi-private room. He did this by arranging many of the lockers around his bunk, and this truly *prized possession* was to be passed down to the next ranking enlisted man. As a showing of gratitude, the lucky soldier that was next in seniority and destined to receive this prize, offered to buy Arie as many drinks as he wanted to consume. Desiring to make a good impression on his new unit, he informed the lucky recipient that he was staying away from any alcohol for a couple of days.

A few days later and with his duffle bag securely on his shoulder, he carefully negotiated the icy steps down to the roadway, for this was the day of his transfer. From the bottom of the steps, it was only a few hundred feet to the main gate where a shiny brown staff car was waiting for him. He was nearly singing out his thoughts of *Sunshine and blue skies—here I come!*

Chapter Five: Into the Fray

What a nice and comfortable ride it was for him, compared to what he normally experienced in either a bus or the back of a canvass-covered truck. Now, here he was sitting alone in the back seat of the big car and being chauffeur-driven to Seoul. Per his usual method of enjoying the ride through Seoul, he looked at as many pretty girls as he could see on the streets. It was now that he noticed groups of soldiers that resembled Koreans and they were wandering the streets in search of the same thing that all soldiers from the beginning of time have sought—available women. The only noticeable differences were the unit designation on the sleeves of their jackets—the designation was Vet Nam. It left him wondering if they were veterans of a battle in a place called Nam. Obviously whoever had come up with the sleeve patch was as unaware of Vietnam as he was, for they did not spell the patch properly. At his final destination, he removed his duffle bag from the car trunk and he remembers entering a small non-discrete building near an airport.

As he entered into a long, well-lit room with approximately a dozen small curtained areas that were evidently for the changing of clothing, there was no one in sight. At the time he called out a simple but firm, "Hello. Anyone here?"

Nearly immediately a man in civilian clothes appeared. That man told him to go into the area behind a specific numbered curtain and to put on the clothes that were there. In Korea, US Army personnel were required to surrender all their civilian clothing and this made him question why is this person wearing civilian clothes and issuing the orders to military personnel? As he started toward the curtain, the man insisted, "Take your bag, because you will need to use your low quarter shoes."

He had to admit even then that he found this whole occurrence to be rather confusing, since previously he had only worn shoes while on leave. Opening the curtain exposed him to an even bigger surprise because on the garment hooks were new civilian clothes! It was against US Army regulations in Korea for soldiers even to own civilian clothes. In time he would come to believe that at the time he was not in Korea, but rather in Thailand or Laos.

With no recourse available to him, he performed as instructed and he dressed in the civilian clothes. He did so without any thought as to how or why they were exactly his size, right down to the 30-inch length of the leg. On the hook beneath the clothes, he discovered a new 35mm camera and leather case. At first, he was apprehensive about touching it, as it was not part of the order he had received and it could possibly be the personal property of another soldier. However, in the end he decided to put the strap over his shoulder and to let them tell him to take it off, if it was not to be a part of his *new uniform*.

Within a short time, he heard a multitude of nervous laughter on the other side of the curtain. He opted to take a peek and he received quite a startle. He stood there gazing in disbelief at approximately a dozen other men dressed in *exactly* the same clothes with *exactly* the same cameras on *exactly* the same shoulder! Ordered to line up with them, he could not resist the impulse to lean forward to look up and down the row at the almost mirror images of himself. Standing at attention, he observed that they were all healthy, straight-backed and early twenties Caucasian men with white sidewall haircuts, white short-sleeve shirts with matching pants, identical shoes and the same cameras without film. He remembers asking himself, “My God, is this the new army that I have heard so much about?”

In a short time, the Major that he had met at First Cavalry Division Headquarters came around the corner, accompanied by a Sergeant and the odd-looking civilian. The Major introduced the civilian as an intelligence officer and as the new commander. The civilian officer began by telling the troupe of soldiers to relax, while he informed them of the destination and the task to which they were now assigned. Below he has tried to capture the gist of that message, and he does so without any attempt of verbatim.

"You men are about to embark on a unique mission—a mission that has been requested by the South Vietnamese President and approved by the US Government. This mission, and your task within it, is to get you quietly into Vietnam, so that you can do your job of training the Montagnard tribesmen. You will find the Montagnards are very much like our own American Indians. They speak a different language and have different ways than the other Vietnamese, but they love their country and are unwilling to allow outsiders to dictate to them what they can or cannot do. Some of these tribes are in dangerous situations and unstable areas, while others are not now threatened, but may be at a later date. Therefore, it goes without saying that some of you may be involved in dangerous duties and you must stay on your toes at all times, especially at night. You will need to tutor the Montagnard tribesmen and prepare them to defend their homeland as quickly as possible. There will be one man allotted to train each tribe, since the tribes are small and we have determined that this will be more than sufficient. There will be a language translator among the tribesmen to assure your orders are properly conveyed. Now in a few hours, you will transfer to a civilian bus as tourists. From the time you board until you are dropped off individually at your destination, you must not salute, say sir, nor give any other indication of ever having any military training. Do you have any questions?"

Being one that was never known to avoid asking the obvious questions, regardless of the nasty consequences to be endured, he raised his hand and asked the single nagging question that was on his mind. "Sir, have you ever seen tourists that were dressed exactly alike? It has been my experience that tourists dress in all manners of clothing and no two of them ever look the same."

"These people have never seen a tourist! You will be in a bus with darkened windows and you will be dropped off out there alone. That being the case there will be no way for them to know that the others are dressed the same as you are dressed. Any other questions?"

Again he raised his hand to ask a pressing question. "Sir, where are the women and kids that are normally seen with tourists? The tribesmen may not have seen tourists, but it can't be said for all the other people that will be observing these movements."

"I believe I have already answered your question, Soldier."

Feeling slightly offended and not to be brushed off so easily, he adds a final remark. "Sir, I believe we can no more pass for tourists than World War II Storm Troopers would have been seen as tourists in New York City! Provided that they were dressed exactly alike—as we are!"

In the years since, he has never been able to recall the reply of the man and it is probably best left unprinted.

After be allowed a few minutes for a drink of water and to perform personal functions, they were quickly marched off single file to board a cargo plane. It was the first time he had ever seen the inside of any plane, so he nervously sat in one of its little canvas seats that was running down each side. They were in short-sleeved white shirts with open collar and not in the least aware of any cold. For most of his life, he assumed they were in a heated and closed airplane hangar.

Later his many civilian experiences, acquired while working on and around aircraft, have proven to him that this could not have been true. Persons that regularly work in hangers during the winter months wear thick-soled shoes and heavy clothes, since the cold permeates through the concrete floor and very little can keep out the chill. Even with all external openings securely closed and the massive heaters running at full blast, it is impossible to keep any hanger at a moderately warm temperature. Therefore, he must have been in a warm climate at the time. He faintly recalls someone saying all of them would fly to Thailand, before going by bus through Laos to South Vietnam.

It seems that titillation filled his very being as the plane door slammed closed and they prepared to embark toward his ultimate destination. Then within a short time, the door opened again with the Sergeant calling out his name. "Stone! Where's Stone?"

He answered, "Here."

The Sergeant immediately and forcefully shoved a clipboard into his chest, while commanding him, "Sign here!"

Taking the clipboard from him, he asked, "What am I to sign?"

The Sergeant calmly replied almost as an afterthought, "It's your re-enlistment papers for more years in the Army."

He bluntly and loudly told him, "There is no way in Hell that I am going to re-enlist!"

The mood of the Sergeant changed and he angrily shouted, “You will if you want an assignment where it’s warm!”

He stubbornly refused to sign the re-enlistment and he emphatically told the sergeant that very fact. “I am willing to go for my remaining six months of duty and not one day more!”

Quickly turning away, the Sergeant whispered something to the glaring civilian. In turn, the civilian screamed, “Then get the hell off this plane, asshole!”

Chapter six: Returned to Base

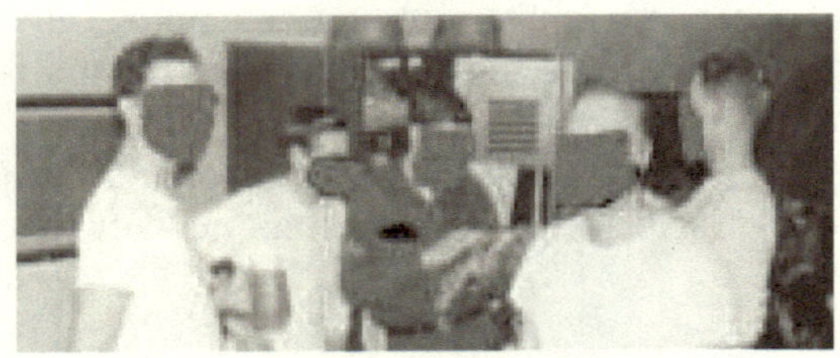

Returning to the office area inside the exceptionally warm hangar, Arie is ordered to change out of the civilian clothes and to put on normal his military outfit, since they are taking him back to his old unit. After doing as he was ordered, he stepped from behind the curtain to find that everyone had gone and the place was empty, except for the Sergeant.

The demeanor of the Sergeant had changed and he quietly asked him, "You want to eat some potato chips and have a cola, prior to the long way back?"

Arie was quite hungry, as he believes that he had not eaten for at least eight hours. He hurriedly stuffed his mouth with chips while drinking the entire cup of cola that was presented to him.

All the while, the Sergeant sat beside him and tried to explain that he understood how the Army was not meant to be a career for some people. He continued for a long time, as he talked about how wonderful the Army has treated him. Then for no apparent reason, the Sergeant shot up out of the seat and walked directly behind Arie instead of taking the shorter route to the only other room. Not at all being the trusting type, Arie instinctively turned in his seat to make sure the Sergeant kept moving and thankfully he did continue.

With the Sergeant temporarily out of the room Arie returned to the eating of the chips, and when he ran out of cola for a second time he helped himself to what remained in the refrigerator. He remembers there were only a few colas, but quite a large quantity of other items, including vials of liquid and four or five palm-sized packages of what appeared to be powdered milk or powdered sugar. It was an interesting array, but he was not concerned, since he had seen similar items in the refrigerator at the Company Pharmacy.

Today many people would say anyone taking in food or drink that is prepared out of their site is a total fool! However you must remember that this event occurred in 1961. At that time, the public's limited knowledge of illegal drugs consisted of their believing that such things must be smoked or injected. Unbeknownst to any regular soldier or to him, the US Government had recently developed LSD for top-secret operations, and it had only been in their arsenal of use for a few years. It would be another five years until its introduction to the drug-induced hallucinations of the Hippie generation, and their ever-popular pass time of *salting* potato chips at parties.

Was it LSD? Who knows! For he surely does not know the answer. All he is positive about is that his life changed, because on that day he changed! Up until that time his life had been fairly organized, allowing him to properly equate that his performing **action A** would result in his receiving **reaction B**. Prior to this time, it was all rather logical and somewhat cut and dried, in his opinion

Many hours or days later in the cold near Seoul, he remembers putting his duffle bag into the back of an open topped jeep, and laughing at the obvious desire of the Army to make him suffer for his refusal to re-enlist. The person in charge intentionally sent two men with him in the topless Jeep, so that Arie would be forced to sit in the back seat and away any possible wind-breaking ability of the small windshield. It was quite a turn-around from the warm car that had brought him to the site, but whatever they threw at him, he could endure even if it meant two hours in frigid winds and extreme cold. For close to an hour, he sat with his duffle bag between his legs and laid his face on it to help shield away some of the freezing wind and cold. Then he must have dozed off asleep.

That is the last he recalls, until they shouted at him. "Get out! You're at the main gate."

Apparently they did not have proper credentials enter the gate even though they were in a US Army jeep, so they had parked nearly 100 feet away. Perhaps they parked that far away to cause him a little more discomfort. He slowly exited the jeep, picked up his duffel bag and made his way back to his hutch. In any event, they sat there watching him until he was within a few feet of the door to the barrack, and then they slowly drove away.

Once inside they place he has hoped to never see again, he told the other soldier to move his stuff out of the semiprivate area, as the transfer was cancelled and he was back to stay. It was very late at night and the other soldier was quite upset, but he complied, and soon Arie fell asleep on the bare mattress.

For quite some time afterward, he often wondered how he had managed to stay in bed for the entire weekend. However he now estimates that he had been gone for two or three days, since his time in bed went by so quickly. Thus he returned to his outfit on a Sunday night rather than the same Friday that he left. Concerned that the other soldiers might pry into his activities, he did not ask any questions about his length of absence.

That Monday morning arrived rather quickly for him and he was greeted warmly and enthusiastically by all, when he reported for duty at his old job. To his surprise, not one Sergeant or Officer ever asked him what he was doing back. He can only conclude that they must have known the official reason. In view of the fact that no paper trail exists, the notification to them must have been made via a simple telephone call. Being a good soldier, Arie always followed orders and so he followed his last instruction to maintain secrecy. He told the other soldiers that he was not accepted for the new assignment simply because he refused to re-enlist. He never told any of them what the new assignment entailed or where he had been for the past few days.

It was during that same week when the nightmares began and they tormented Arie for months. At first he would wake up screaming for his "Daddy," to the laughter and taunts of the other sleepy soldiers. Then the fun wore off with their sleep broken up nearly every night by "Corporal Crazy." At least that is what they began to call him behind his back. Each morning his bedding would be wet with perspiration, as he fought off his loving God, the North Koreans and many others that in his nightmares would continually threaten his life. Once he dreamed that God, in a white shirt and dark trousers, was trying to kill him by squeezing his chest, as a boa would tighten the grasp on his victim with every exhale. Gasping until awake, he could not imagine that God would do such a thing! At the time, the term flashback did not exist to explain such memory relapses. Thus he rationalized that it was really his father or grandfather and not God that was trying to kill him. This is what he has believed for many years, and he still considers it a valid possibility. Today he has come to accept that most probably it was the image of the out of place CIA civilian that was tormenting his sleep.

A month after returning to his old outfit and while off post drinking, one of his sergeants became completely incapacitated from an enormous intake of alcohol. Although the man was twice the size of Arie, he put him on his back and carried him the entire mile back to camp. The guards at the gate simply laughed and motioned him on with his heavy load. After putting the inebriated sergeant to bed, Arie went to his bunk and immediately fell asleep.

Within an hour or so, there was suddenly a painfully bright light in his blood shot eyes and he instinctively pushed it away. As his eyes became able to focus, he could see that it was the same sergeant that he had carried back to base and the man was standing over him cursing like a maniac! Nothing Arie said helped the situation as the Sergeant promised to make his life miserable, starting at that very moment.

After a few minutes the Sergeant gave him an order. “Get dressed and pick up any trash that is around the building.”

Arie protested, “But Sarge, it’s 2 A.M. and I have to get up at 4:30!”

It made no difference and the Sergeant kept him out there for more than an hour. This was just the beginning, as he had Arie on every disgusting chore that he could imagine, until the time when the Sergeant was finally transferred back to the States.

With his nemesis now gone, the month of March in its turn was strangely a blessing, as Arie was in disbelief that he could survive the previous month. Encouraged, he now took all kinds of things into stride: karate classes, weight lifting, the study of German and even the challenge to quit smoking.

The Germanic language is tough for anyone to learn, but Arie just could not understand why it did not come to him rather easily. In his altered mind he had begun to believe that he was the reincarnation of a German Army Sergeant killed during the initial attack upon Russia. However, the German language continued to evade his understanding and it does so to this day.

The one item that put him through even more Hell was his decision that after eleven years of smoking he would simply quit. In the slum where he was raised, most children started smoking and sometimes chewing as soon as they realized that is what adults do to socialize. He picked up the habit of regularly smoking when he was around eight years of age. However his quitting took six weeks of gut-wrenching turmoil to give up the nasty habit. In time he did successfully accomplish that very difficult task by late March and he was able to quit forever.

Why he took on so very much and at the same time, he does not know. He does know that it was not because he was being castigated by his peers as a loner, although he was most assuredly being ostracized. Arie had learned at an early age that true leaders are by necessity loners. In the third grade, he had assembled every male student in the second through fourth grades into his supposed gang, with his older brother as Second-in-Command. He only disbanded the group of more than 400 boys when there was no one else remaining to coerce into joining.

The Army seemed to recognize this ability in him too. They offered him a chance to go to Officers Candidate School to become a Second Lieutenant, but circumstances involved with his enlistment age caused him to refuse. He had forged his birth date in order to enter the Military, and a birth certificate would have been required for acceptance as an officer. In support of his refusal, the Company Commander made him pay and pay for what was considered a wrong decision! For twenty-two days in a row he was put on Kitchen Police and required to work from 4 AM to 10 PM.

Chapter Seven: Touring North Korea

Early one morning in April, as he returned to the Guard Shack after pulling another tour along the DMZ, an Army ambulance pulled up beside him. Suddenly the back doors popped open allowing him to see inside, where there were two rifle totting soldiers, plus a Staff Sergeant with a side arm.

The Sergeant immediately jumped out and asked him, "You want to go with us?"

Since they were a group of strangers, Arie felt it was necessary to ask, "Where to?"

He received only an incomprehensible and vague answer from the Sergeant. However he decided to go anyway. He realizes now that it could have been a fatalistic response, and even at the time, he wondered whether he was in fact being arrested for some reason. Nevertheless, he got into the back and they went off down the dirt roads to wherever the driver was planning to go. The driver appeared drugged or for some reason in a robotic state and he was unwilling to take suggestions from any of them in the back. The sole person responsible for issuing instructions was the Sergeant.

After a short time, while sitting close to the rear door's window, Arie could see they were heading for the "Bridge of No Return," which separates South Korea from North Korea.

In any event, across it they went and continued north toward Panmunjom. Due to the bouncing of the military ambulance, the photos taken by Arie are not very clear.

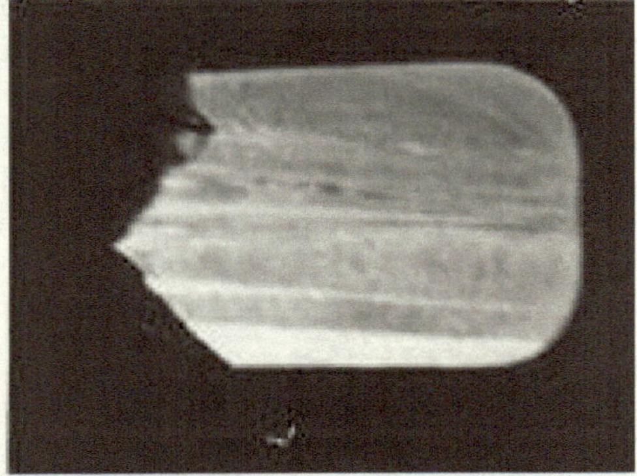

For some reason unknown that was never explained to him, they did not stop in the United Nations side of Panmunjom. Instead they simply seemed to wander about the North Korean countryside, until being spotted by an enemy Lieutenant. Arie could not resist, so he took a photo of the North Korean officer through the window and he has retained that photo.

At any rate, in his fatalistic emotional condition he laughed at the possibility of their being caught on the wrong side of the border and with a loaded weapon. However, the other soldiers were visibly shaken and whatever plan they had in mind was quickly put aside in favor of an immediate return to the US lines of defense. In about an hour, they were again south of the border where the driver dropped him off at the guard shack and drove away quickly. He had never seen any of them previously and he never saw them after that incident. None of them ever introduced themselves, and they always seemed to stay together as a team. Of course they all left together in the ambulance, just as they had arrived. With the First Cavalry Division spread over a multitude of small camps, it is odd that in the headquarters camp of about 500 personnel, he had no recollection of ever meeting any one of them before or since the trip.

Today he believes that his going along with them was rather naive, as it could well have been a plot to get rid of a potential problem by simply dropping him on the wrong side of the border. He was armed with a loaded rifle, and it is improbable that he would ever have been heard from again. Certainly the US Military at the time was adept at denying any knowledge of soldiers that ended up on the wrong side of the Korean border. However if by some fortuitous circumstance he did manage to return, it is illogical to assume that he could have made it back by the time he was due for another tour of guard duty. Therefore, he would have been declared a deserter. Either of the presented scenarios could have cleared up the perceived problem that he may have been to whoever was responsible for the actions of those in the ambulance.

While he knew there simply had to be a deeper reason for his fatalistic attitude toward life, at the time he had no idea what the source was behind his actions.

It was about this time that he began mentally to question the high number of personnel files that were being gathered for soldiers serving in the First Cavalry Division that died while in Korea. Quietly investigating, he found that during the previous 12 months there was only one soldier that died of the infamous tick bite of which all soldiers were so frequently warned to beware. Meanwhile, seventeen or more had died from "playing quick draw" with other soldiers! In one case, both a Sergeant and another soldier supposedly killed each other during such a contest. Arie was only nineteen at the time and even now he laughs at the audacity of such claims. He had been in Korea for nearly a full year without ever hearing a single soldier mention playing quick draw, or challenging another soldier to such a match or thus far knowing someone that had exhibited a desire to engage in such a stupid competition. All of them were aware of the need for extreme care when handling weapons and even when drunk they would not have considered performing such a flagrant violation of good soldierly conduct! Yet the families of these soldiers were informed of their deaths at the hands of other soldiers. He did not accept it as a fact then and he does not accept it as fact today!

A few nights after his excursion into North Korea, his anger inexplicably boiled over and he tried to find someone to fight. However, the bar was nearly empty and his insane raving caused it to completely empty within a minute or so. Even the bartender refused to have anything to do with him, and the bar was closed early to avoid any further encounter. With nothing left to do, Arie walked the 390 stair steps back down the hill toward his hut.

He does not know whether it was his taking on too much at one time, or what it was that caused him to snap, but snap he did! He karate-chopped one of the wooden guardrails and it split like an over-ripe watermelon. He chopped another, then another and then went back to the very top of the stairs, where he started to destroy every one of them. It was as though he was at war and surrounded by the enemy. In the end, he took great delight in destroying all 300 feet of the handrails and making sure that not one single rail was left standing!

The next morning, as he looked up the hill and at the utter destruction, it appeared as though a tornado had been there. He was appalled that he could do such an insane thing. He did not know why he would even consider doing such an act, as he never had been the destructive type, because he knew that some good people had put in a lot of effort into building these items. Although, it looked like a whirlwind had ripped through the area, there was absolutely no mention of the incident by anyone. He watched and waited in amazement that no reward was offered, and no request was ever made for information on the responsible culprit. Further, his act of rage was well within sight of the Military Police Post and they must have heard the racket, as the noise would have travelled quite a distance in the hush of the late night. To this day, he does not understand why the Army chose simply to ignore the act. Yet he took a photo to document the rage that he was feeling, and of course he has that photo also.

Chapter Eight: From the Army to Hell

After returning home to the Midwest in July 1961, he told a modified version about the mission to most of his family, but not one of them had ever heard of Laos or Viet Nam. The one thing he did not tell them was that there was a small piece of his life that was somehow blanked out. He attributed most of his actions simply to not adjusting to being out of the Military and that was why he was drinking heavily, while intermittently dating some lovely young women. Today he is not sure he was being truthful to himself, but then he was only a month past his twentieth birthday. Perhaps it was merely youthful exuberance.

A few weeks after being home, he went to bed with everything appearing to be normal. The next morning he awoke completely nude on his left side, but fully and neatly dressed on his right side including still having on the right sock and shoe. Not knowing what else to do, he simply laughed the matter off.

The year 1961 was not being good to him, and he could feel that he was becoming more fatalistic in everything he did. Today his situation would probably be labeled Post-traumatic-stress (PTSD), but not at that time as most persons in situations similar to his were simply expected to recover on their own from the half-craziness that seemingly possessed them.

It should be noted that drinking and fighting was a way of life in his neighborhood, as it had always been, and he fit in very well with that standard of conduct. One night an attacker followed him to the home of an older brother and there Arie was assailed by what looked to him to be a pistol. It turned out to be a piece of lead pipe that resembled the barrel of a revolver and the man got in one good hit with it across his mouth before he took it from him and beat in his head. Similar to poking a stick into the belly of a sleeping bear, the aggressor caused him to become infuriated at the audacity of the act. Moments later as the aggressor begged on his knees for him to spare his life, Arie continued to smash his head and drive the face of the man into the dirt, until his brother could pull him off. Later his Sister-in-law said that she had never seen anyone with such hatred in the eyes of anyone as what she had witnessed being exhibited that night. He surmises that he most certainly did try to kill the person, possibly because the man somehow reminded him of the Sergeant from the CIA incident. The newspaper article he has in his possession reveals that the person required 28 stitches to his mangled scalp and not the 90 stitches reported to him by the police. No charges were filed against Arie, since the other man was the aggressor.

Reports Cuts in Tire Tool Attack

A local man suffered four cuts on the head Tuesday night, allegedly inflicted by another man using a tire tool.

After being home for only about six weeks, Arie became engaged to the wonderful neighbor girl that had so faithfully awaited his return. Barely 60 days later, they were married and they stayed married until her death. The day they married, made him realize that he was truly, truly happy for the first time ever! That Christmas Eve, he lay in bed watching the tree lights flicker and he never wanted the night to end. On that most magnificent of nights, he was warm, dry, safe and with the one young woman in the whole world that truly loved him. As an added bonus, she had recently told him that they were to have their first child in the fall. He was so happy that tears rolled down his cheeks. As she slept in his arms, all he could think was that *life is so wonderful!* All the same, he was not really a part of the human race at that time and certainly not worthy of her, nor would he be worthy for quite some time.

A couple of months into their life together, his wife thought it would be funny to jump on him as he left the bathroom and re-entered the totally darkened bedroom. It was nearly a fatal mistake that he has never forgotten, because he had the urge to kill his attacker. He only found out his error, as he began to choke her and realized the skin was too soft and smooth to be the skin of a man.

Whatever the reasons, his reactions to other instances were to become a well-known and often shunned matter of family record.

In his lifetime he had never been a sleepwalker, as his wife was known to be. His sister had warned him that his wife walked in her sleep, but he had no intention of letting something so trivial keep him from marrying such a goddess.

That next fall his nightmares came back vigorously, and over the next two years his wife found him doing strange things in his sleep. At this time the only thing that could wake him was someone calling his name, and then he would awake as he answered the person. He must assume that as a youngster he was trained in this manner to wake up by his mother calling his name, as she was waking him for school.

The first nightmare found him on the drafty floor, freezing and asking for some cover. Only when he heard his wife call out his name did he awake.

"Arie, where are you?"

She turned on the light and found him in a fetal position on the cold floor. After getting him back in bed she hugged him for nearly an hour, until he stopped shaking and his teeth quieted down.

The problems continued with her frequently waking him, as later he walked repeatedly into the bedroom wall, while trying to exit the bedroom.

The third time was much worse, when she called, "Arie, come back to bed."

He informed her, "I am in bed, but this mattress sure is hard and uncomfortable tonight!"

Getting out of bed, she found him standing straight up against the wall!

He could not explain why he was acting this way, and he was terribly embarrassed that he had done such ridiculous things in front of his new wife. To this day, he is amazed that she loved him too much to leave him alone with his many problems.

After being satisfied that things were finally coming together, nothing could have prepared him for the experience that occurred a few months prior to his twenty-third birthday. His requirement to be in the office by six each morning usually meant that he would go to bed around eight o'clock, while his wife and their young child continued watching TV.

One night he was having a very nice dream, when suddenly Saint Peter commanded that he come to him, and slowly the spirit of Arie began to exit his body. He was shocked at what was happening, as he could see his wife and child through the bottom of the floor even while he was evidently leaving them forever! Emphatically shouting, “No,” he pulled himself back into his body. Then he found that he was mostly paralyzed on his left side. Unable to speak or to move, he lay there in panic for more than half an hour grunting and groaning, until his prayers were answered and his wife opened the door to see what was wrong. She lovingly held him in her arms as he tried to tell her the story, but his face was numb and only the right side of his body worked. Drooling as he tried to speak, he could not control his lips on the left side of his face nor even open his left eye, and he stayed that way for hours. The next morning he did not attempt to go to work, since the left side of his face was only partially responding. It would be a few more days before he would return to being physically normal. Despite everything, the emotional scars of whatever caused this trauma will remain with him to the end of his days.

Then after three or four years of normality, the same things began to happen at places other than at home. On one occasion at about four-thirty in the morning, he heard his name being called out. Only then did he realize that he was at work. He stood there horrified with a trembling body and with his knees weakened. He grabbed his belt for some measure of reassurance, for he knew if he had a belt on then it would make sense that he had on his pants also. He was so relieved that he was not nude in public! For a man such as he, known to profess being afraid of nothing and no one, he was forced to admit that waking up unclothed in public was a severely frightening thought.

How could he tell his wife? Previously she had awoken in the middle of the night to find him nude and sleeping on the floor in the fetal position. What was next? On this occasion, he was very fortunate in being fully dressed. Evidently he had performed all his usual morning tasks, including shaving and showering.

Subsequently as he looked around trying to distinguish friend from foe, he managed a slight smile at whoever it was that called his name. Then he realized that he was in the well-lit hallway near his office, and it was another employee that had simply said, "Good morning, Arie." Leaning against a chair to regain his composure, he quickly explained to his friend that it must be a sinus problem that was making him dizzy.

In a few minutes the excessive perspiration slowed and he went to his office where he waited until eight in the morning. He wanted to be sure that his wife was wide-awake prior to calling her and asking about his events. Perplexed by his own actions, he informed her that for some unknown reason he had arrived at work four hours early. He had to ask her to tell him what she remembered, and that caused her to be understandably worried. How can any man get out of bed, shave, bathe, eat breakfast, kiss his family goodbye and drive eight miles to work without ever knowing what he was doing? Was he on the edge mental collapse? Was a nervous breakdown in the offing? You can bet that Arie had the utmost concern about his future!

Unfortunately this was not to be the last time that he had such an unpleasant experience. For ten long and unmerciful years, whatever caused his problems had had him feeling on the verge of lunacy. These actions would continue for another half dozen times prior to ceasing permanently.

To this day he does not know what instigated his problem or why the problem subsequently went away. However he does have his suspicions and those lay with his volunteering for this CIA Mission to an internal hell.

The end.

Epilogue

What Arie has recited here is only a small part of his story—a story that he was greatly reluctant to reveal out of respect for his family. Unusual things, and random thoughts of things most bizarre, would persist to haunt him for nearly forty-five years. Even at this late date, it hurts him to know that all this may have happened simply because he was trying to be a good soldier—a good soldier with inner dreams of perhaps becoming another decorated hero in the country that he so dearly loves.

Yet he cannot correlate to the highest degree of certainty exactly what took place after his leaving the assigned camp to go on this mission. Often though, he continues to wonder what in actual fact did happen to the other soldiers who bravely volunteered for that infamous mission—soldiers that were as much strangers to him as he was to them. Their fate appears to be known only to God and to a select few individuals on this Earth. He suspects that no more than a small number of those daring volunteers—if any—ever returned home to their loving families. They were young and vibrant men that were quite possibly wiped from existence as they tried to perform an admirable endeavor for their country.

Firmly believing there were many more instances of this nature, the Author is anxious to hear from any person that took part in similar operations to train the Montagnards in Southeast Asia, or from the survivors of soldiers that died under mysterious circumstances or somehow disappeared while stationed in Korea or Southeast Asia during 1960 though 1962.

Please supply the name of the service person, dates of service and other pertinent information to this Author via the publisher.

www.ingramcontent.com/pod-product-compliance
Lightning Source LLC
LaVergne TN
LVHW041301150826
845673LV00008B/2687

* 9 7 9 8 7 5 1 8 3 3 3 0 5 *